Table of Contents

Frank DeLima's Joke Book

Edited by Jerry Hopkins

Having fun with Portagees, Pakes,
Buddha Heads, Buk Buks, Blallahs,
Soles, Yobos, Haoles, Tidahs, Pit Bulls,
and other Hawaiian minorities

Bess Press
P. O. Box 22388
Honolulu, HI 96823

Frank DeLima would like to acknowledge Patrick Downes for assistance with many of the songs. Also: Tremaine Tamayose for "Bruce Spring Roll" and Dave Donnelly for "Korea."

Cover design: Paula Newcomb

Photographs: Photoplant/Ray Tanaka

DeLima, Frank
    Frank DeLima's Joke Book
Honolulu, Hawaii: Bess Press, Inc.
112 pages

ISBN: 0-935848-97-5

INTRODUCTION

I visit every public school in the state of Hawaii every year, and every private school every two years. I am not an expert and I don't have all the answers, but at each school, I tell the kids three things. I say that there are three important things in life.

The first thing I say is to study and to read. By reading and studying and staying in school, and by enjoying school, you will gain an open mind about life and people. In that way, you will have an easier time dealing with life and people you come into contact with. Also, a good education gets you a good job.

The second thing is family. Family means to help, not to hurt. To respect people, especially those who love and care for you---parents, teachers and those in authority like policemen, firemen, and doctors, people who are there to help our society. Also, respect your schoolmates and your brothers and sisters, by playing nicely, never to hurt but to help. Talk nicely to others. Never gossip. Never say things in anger. Family means to help, not to hurt.

The third thing is laughing. I believe that laughter is the key to happiness. It releases pressure. It makes you feel good. You cannot frown when you laugh. And you cannot feel bad when you laugh. I guarantee it. Laughter makes a happy heart.

Especially if you can laugh at yourself. Here in Hawaii, we laugh at ourselves more than most people do in other places. Hawaii is a chop suey nation--Portagee, Pake, Buddha Head, Sole, Yobo, Kanaka, Haole, all mixed up. Nobody is in the majority here. We are all part of at least one minority group. Some of us are part of several minority groups. And we all laugh at ourselves. This is healthy.

Most people in the world think that there is nothing wrong with their ethnic group--that it is flawless. Most times, they are not exposed to other ethnic groups when they are growing up. A Korean growing up in Korea is in the majority. Same thing with Japanese in Japan, and Samoans in Samoa. Because they are in the majority, what they do seems normal. When they move from their country and come to places like Hawaii, where there are people from many other places, that doesn't make their behavior wrong, only different.

And sometimes differences are funny. It is not cruel to have fun with these differences. Those who take offense cause problems. Those who accept that they are different and have fun with it, create harmony. To have fun with these differences, however, takes sensitivity--especially if you are a joketeller.

There are four things to know about telling jokes--according to DeLima.

Number one, you have to know why you are telling a joke. It is specifically to make people laugh. You should have a happy heart when telling jokes. Those who tell jokes specifically to hurt, or to get back out of anger, or to intentionally degrade someone, these people are misusing humor and they are grossly wrong.

Number two, you have to be sensitive to whom you are telling jokes to. A professional like myself has a green light to tell jokes in public when asked to perform. However, even I, as a professional, offstage will not go up to a Japanese tourist, for example, and sing "Slant Eyes" or tell a Japanese joke. That person will not know who I am and definitely will be offended, even if he or she has a sense of humor. Even those people who know who I am, but do not agree with my humor, or my sense of humor, or my material, I should have respect for. I should not impose my humor on them away from my stage.

Number three, be aware of when and where you tell a joke. Timing is important. There are times when laughter is inappropriate.

Number four, you should know what to tell. For a professional, every audience is different. So you have to know which jokes to choose. You must always be sensitive to your audience.

I have been telling jokes for many years. I tell them onstage. I tell them when I visit the schools. Over the years, I have heard hundreds of jokes. Everywhere I go, people tell me jokes. Jokes about Portagees, and Pakes, and Buddha Heads, and Blallahs and Tidahs and Haoles. They are collected here in the spirit of good fun, along with some of my favorite songs--songs I have recorded and performed onstage.

If you are offended by any of these jokes or songs, I apologize. It is not my intention to offend. But I also ask you to look at why you are offended. Are you taking something too personally? Are you taking yourself too seriously?

Being able to laugh at yourself is healthy. In fact, many doctors today say laughter can heal. So consider this a book about improving your health.

Laugh. Enjoy. Feel good about yourself. Don't be so uptight. Hang loose.

DA PORTAGEE

The Portuguese March

Let's give three cheers for all the Portuguese
From Clyde Guerrero to Carlene Moniz
Let's give a toast to Jimmy Mendoza
Leroy Fernandez and Marie Ortiz
And then we gladly will extend our hand
To all the Freitases throughout the land
To every Figueroa big and small
We raise our glasses to you all

To Tony Souza let's extend our praise
To Sue Rapoza let our voices raise
For George Correa and his dear wife Judy
For June Machado let the beacons blaze
Let all the trumpets sound for Liz Jardine
Let's put Gouveia on *Time* magazine
For every Olivera in the world
Let the banners be unfurled

For Bill DeMello let the sirens blare
For Jim Perrera burst the bombs in air
Let's launch a ship called the Norma Gonzalves
For George Brilhante let the rockets flare
For Rose Pacheco let the armies march
Above her birthplace build a golden arch
On every Espinoza that we know
A million honors we bestow

For Pearl DeLima let the saints appear
And Bob Medeiros let the world revere
Let's throw a party for Francis Robello
And let's invite the northern hemisphere
For Joe Farias let the sun eclipse
And then commence with the apocalypse

Hip, hip, hurrah for Portugal!
Hip, hip, hurrah for Portugal!
Hip, hip, hurrah for Portugal!

NOTE: When the Portuguese came to the islands to work on the plantations, the Hawaiians tried to pronounce "Portuguese "and couldn't. It came out "Portagees." That's what we're stuck with. Portagees.

Hawaiian Telephone Company was trying out three small firms to see which one could bury the most telephone poles in a day. The winner would get a large contract.

The hard-working haole company buried 30 poles in one eight-hour day. The man from the phone company was impressed, until the Pake company reported 40 poles erected. Last, the Portagee firm came in and Manuel said they had buried four poles.

"Is that all?" the boss asked. "The haole company buried 30 poles and the Pake company buried 40 poles and you only buried four?"

"Well!" said Manuel. "Look how many they left sticking out of the ground."

Did you hear about the time Manuel went ice fishing and brought home 100 pounds of ice?

And his wife drowned trying to cook it?

A local guy was sitting on his porch when he saw Joaquin, his Portagee neighbor, circling the block for two hours. Finally he went to the corner and waited for Joaquin to come around again. When Joaquin did, he yelled out, "Hey, what's a matter with you? You been driving around the block for two hours."

Joaquin stopped his car, stuck his head out of the car window and yelled back, "My blinker stuck!"

What does it say on the top of a Portagee ladder?

STOP!

Why do Portagees have broad shoulders and flat heads?

Because when you ask them a question [shrug your shoulders] they shrug their shoulders, and when you tell them the answer [slap your forehead] they slap their heads and say, "Auwe, why didn't I think of that?!"

Why don't Portagees think Polack jokes are funny?

Because it sounds like what they do all day.

Did you hear about the Portagee who heard on the radio that 90 percent of all accidents happen within a 10-mile radius of home?

He moved.

Did you hear about the Portagee doctor who perfected a new surgical procedure?

He performed the first hernia transplant.

A Portagee family was driving along the Wailua River toward the beach in a pickup truck. Mom and Dad were in the truck and the three kids were in the back. Suddenly the right front tire blew out and the truck veered into the river and sank. Mom and Dad emerged from the cabin and swam toward the river bank. After pulling themselves onto the dry land, they looked back at where the truck had gone down, expecting to see their children swimming behind them. Several minutes went by and just as they had decided the kids had drowned, their heads bobbed to the surface. When finally they floundered to the shore, their parents asked, "What happened? What took you guys so long?"

Still gasping for breath, one of the children explained, "We couldn't get the tailgate down."

Manuel and Joaquin were at the funeral of one of their friends.

"He sure looks good," said Manuel.

"He should," said Joaquin. "He just got out of the hospital."

Do you know why landscape gardeners won't employ Portagees?

When they put down a new lawn, the guy in charge has to keep shouting, "Green side up! Green side up!"

Manuel applied for a job at the Honolulu Police Department. He was given test after test and he failed them all. The City wanted to have a Portagee on the force and so they gave him one more test. This one had only one question: "Who shot President Kennedy?"

Manuel said, "I don't know." "Look," said the Captain, "take this question home and study it. Maybe when you come back tomorrow you'll have the answer."

That night, Manuel's friends asked him if he got the job.

"I think so," he said. "They got me working on a murder case already."

Why do Portagee dogs have flat noses?

From chasing parked cars.

Did you hear about the Portagee whose wife had triplets?

He went out looking for the other two guys.

Two Portagees went to Alaska on vacation and decided to try ice fishing. They stood at their spot for about an hour and didn't even get a bite. One of them walked about a hundred yards to where some Eskimos were pulling them in one right after the other.

When he returned, his friend said, "What are they doing different?"

The first Portagee said, "Well, for one thing, they cut a hole in the ice."

Did you hear about the Portagee who was so stupid that other Portagees noticed?

What did the Portagee call his pet zebra?

Spot.

The minister was disappointed when his mainly Portagee board turned down his request for a chandelier for the church. When he asked why, the board spokesperson said, "Well, for one thing, the secretary can't spell it. For another, nobody knows how to play it, so that would be a waste of money. And another thing, if we're going to spend any money, it should be for a light over the pulpit so you can see better."

How can you tell when a firing squad is made up of Portagees?

It stands in circle.

Freddie Babooze got a job working in a lumber yard. The first day, he was told to join a group of men unloading 2 by 4's from a truck. The foreman noticed that the other men were carrying four timbers at one time, but Freddie was carrying only one. He asked why. Freddie snorted and said, "I can't help it if those other guys are too lazy to make more trips."

Why don't Portagees play hide and seek?

Nobody wants to find them.

How many Portagees does it take to paint a house?

Five thousand and one. One to hold the paint brush and five thousand to turn the house.

Did you hear about the fire that destroyed the Portagee library?

Both books were burned up and one of them hadn't even been colored in yet.

Manuel went up to his friend Joaquin with a big bag in his hand and said, "Joaquin, if you can guess how many chickens I have in this bag, I'll give you both of them."
Joaquin gave it some thought and finally said, "Three?"
Manuel looked disappointed and said, "No fair-- you peeked."

9

If a Portagee throws a pin at you, what should you do?

Run! Because the grenade in his mouth will explode any second.

How many Portagees does it take to make popcorn?

Eleven. One to hold the pan and ten to shake the stove.

Manuel and Joaquin were working for Hawaiian Telephone and were told to measure one of the poles. So Manuel took the measuring tape and climbed up the pole. Joaquin was holding the tape at the bottom.
Pretty soon a haole came walking by and he asked, "What are you doing?"
Joaquin said, "Measuring the pole."
The haole laughed and said, "You should have measured it before you put it up." And then he walked on.
Manuel came down the pole and asked, "What he say?"
Joaquin said, "He said we should have measured it before we put it up."
Manuel said, "Well, the joke's on him. We have to measure the height, not the width!

How can you tell a Portagee car?

When you turn on the ignition, the sound it makes is Pacheco Pacheco Pacheco. When you toot the horn, it goes Arrugia Arrugia Arrugia. And the color of the car is Silva.

Did you hear about the Portagee terrorist who tried to blow up TheBus?

He burned his lips on the exhaust pipe.

Fredddie Babooze entered a pizza shop and ordered a pepperoni pizza. When it came out of the oven, the attendant asked if he wanted it cut into four pieces or eight.
Freddie said, "Make it four. I'll never be able to eat eight."

Did you hear about the Portagee who had body odor only on one side?

He didn't know where to buy Left Guard.

Masa was always playing jokes on Manuel. So Masa tells Manuel, "I know what's going to happen at the end of this cowboy movie."

Manuel goes, "What, Masa?"

And Masa goes, "The cowboy is going get on his horse and ride off into the sunset, hit a tree, fall off the horse, and die."

Manuel goes, "How you know dat?" Masa goes, "I know, brah, I bet you five bucks right now."

So Manual goes, "Shoot, brah." So, they watching the movie and at the end of the movie the cowboy gets on his horse, rides off into the sunset, hits a tree, falls off the horse and dies.

Well, Manuel, in amazement, he turns to Masa, he says, "You smart, you. Here's the five bucks. You won."

Masa says, "Nah, Manuel, I cannot take the money from you."

Manuel says, "Why, you told me the cowboy going die, he died?"

And Masa says, "I know, Manuel, but I seen this movie before."

And Manuel goes, "Oh, me too, but I didn't think the guy would do the stupid thing twice."

Did you hear about the Portagee who wanted to be buried at sea?

It never happened, because all his friends died digging the grave.

Did you hear about the Portagee who put Odor-Eaters in his shoes, walked three steps and disappeared?

Three guys been drifting in a boat, they been drifting for three years. One Hawaiian, one Pake, and one Portagee.

One bottle came by and the Hawaiian open the cork and one genie came out, gave each one of them a wish.

The Hawaiian was first. He said, "Well, brah, I like go back Hawaii and t'row one big luau, last six years, and I invite all my family and friends." His wish was granted and he got back to Hawaii and t'rew one big luau.

The second guy in the boat was one Pake. He said, "I like go back to China and become big kung fu star." Well, his wish was granted and he became one big kung fu star.

The last one on the boat is one Portagee. He look around and the genie say, "What you want, name your wish."

He say, "I wish my friends be back with me."

Did you hear about the Portagee who burned his lips bobbing for french fries?

Manuel and Joaquin were walking down the street and Manuel said, "Look at that dead bird."

Joaquin looked up in the sky and said, "Where?"

A man started telling a joke to someone he met at a party, saying, "Have you heard the Portagee joke about. . . ?"

The second man interrupted and said, "I have to tell you, I'm Portuguese."

"That's okay," said the first man, "I'll tell it slowly."

A Portagee cop stops a speeder on Keeaumoku Street and starts to write out the ticket. He discovers he doesn't know how to spell Keeaumoku. He asks the driver if he'll drive up to King Street and let him stop him again.

A Portagee race driver entered the Indianapolis 500 and made 75 pit stops: three for gas and oil and tire changes, and 72 to ask for directions.

Did you hear about the Portagee who won a gold medal in the Olympic Games?

He had it bronzed.

Manuel was looking for work. He walked up to a house and asked the owner if he had any odd jobs that needed doing. The homeowner said the porch at the rear of the house needed painting. They agreed on a price and the man gave Manuel a brush and a bucket of paint.

A little while later, Manuel returned to the front door and said the job was done. After being paid, and as he was walking away, Manuel said, "By the way, that isn't a Porsche, it's a Lincoln."

The Portagee gym teacher told his students, "Okay, line up alphabetically according to height."

What do you find at the bottom of a bottle of Portagee soda?

The words "Open Other End."

Freddie Babooze took a short cut through the cemetery one night on his way home from the bar and fell into an open grave. A little while later Manuel passed by and heard Freddie moaning. Manuel went over to the grave and looked down.
"What's a matter?" Manuel asked.
"Ohhhhh, I'm so cold," Freddie said.
"Well, no wonder," said Manuel, "you kicked all the dirt off."

What's black, charred, and hangs from a chandelier?

A Portagee electrician.

Did you hear about the Portagee Airlines plane that crashed?

It ran out of coal.

Manuel and Joaquin were walking in Kalihi when a big pigeon flew over and dropped a "prize" on Joaquin's head. Manuel went into a nearby house and came running out with a roll of toilet paper.

"Forget it," said Joaquin, "that pigeon is probably five miles away from here by now."

Why does the Portagee navy have glass-bottomed boats?

So they can see the old Portagee navy.

Joaquin came home early from work and found his wife with another man. He was so upset, he went to the dresser and pulled out his gun and held it to his head.

His wife Mary cried out, "Don't, Joaquin, don't!"

"Oh, yeah!" Joaquin said. "Well, you just wait. You're next!"

Did you hear about the hotel designed by a Portagee architect?

He put the revolving restaurant in the basement.

Did you hear about the Portagee who tried to hijack a submarine?

He demanded $100,000 and a parachute.

Joaquin went into a rent-all shop to rent a saw because he wanted to cut some trees behind his house. The clerk brought out a chain saw and told Joaquin, "This cut those trees in a hurry."

Joaquin took the saw home, but he didn't have any luck. The next day he went back to the rent-all shop with the chain saw. He told the clerk, "This saw doesn't work. All day I cut and cut, but no work." The clerk looked puzzled, but took the saw and pulled the starter rope.

Suddenly Joaquin said, "What's that noise?"

Maria Tunta went to the airport and asked for a round-trip ticket.

"Where to?" the ticket clerk asked.

"Why, back here, of course," Maria said.

A panhandler went up to Freddie Babooze and asked, "Will you give me 50 cents for a sandwich?"

Freddie said, "I don't know. Let me see the sandwich."

Manuel decided he wanted to work for the City-- good job, plenty holidays, lots of benefits. So he filled out the application. Where it asked him to put in his date of birth and the year, he wrote:

Date: July 1

Year: Every year

Did you hear about the Portagee bank robber who walked into a bank, put a $20 bill on the counter and demanded, "Give me all of your brown paper bags!"

The teacher asked little Maria to count to five. She smiled and proudly counted to five on her fingers.

"Very good," said the teacher. "Now, Maria, can you count any higher than that?"

Maria smiled and raised her hand over her head and counted to five again.

Senator Freddie Babooze and Senator Won Ton Chun were discussing some proposed legislation.

Won Ton asked Freddie, "What do you think we should do with the prostitution bill?"

Freddie said, "I think we should pay it."

How can you tell when it's a Portagee parachute?

It opens on impact.

Manuel went to the doctor. After a long examination, the doctor said, "Take these pills two days running, then skip a day. Do this for two weeks, then give me a call." At the end of the first week, Manuel went back to the doctor. "I'm tired, doc," he complained. "I don't mind the running, but the skipping wears me out."

Manuel and Joaquin were putting siding on a house. Manuel was pulling nails from a box and throwing half away.

Joaquin watched Manuel. He scratch his head. Finally he ask, "Manuel, why you throwing all those nails away?"

Manuel, he say, "Heads on 'em pointing wrong way."

Joaquin say, "Stupid you! Those are for other side of house."

Freddie Babooze arrived at work at eleven and his boss shouted, "You should have been here two hours ago!"

Freddie said, "Why? What happened?"

A customer went into a fast food restaurant and said, "I want two hot dogs--one with mustard, one without."

Joaquin, the counterman, said, "Which one?"

How come Portagees don't like M&Ms?

They're too hard to peel.

Did you know that Adam was a Portagee?

Who else would stand beside a naked woman in the Garden of Eden and eat an apple?

Why did the Portagee water half of his lawn?

He heard there was a fifty percent chance of rain.

Did you hear about the Portagee in Kalihi who moved his house fifty feet to take up the slack in the clothesline?

Freddie Babooze worked hard for his company and as a reward got a job in Personnel.   The first day on the new job, he asked the first applicant, "What was your major in college?"

"Mathematics," the applicant answered.

"Well," said Freddie, "that's very good. So say something in mathematics."

"Pi R Square," he replied.

Freddie slapped his knee and laughed. "Boy, are you dumb!" he said. "Pie are round, corn bread are square."

Why do Portagees have TGIF printed on their shoes?

It means "Toes Go In First."

Manuel and Joaquin tried to walk their mule into the barn, but the mule's ears were too long and they hit the top of the door, so the mule refused to enter. After some discussion, Manuel and Joaquin decided to jack up the barn.

They had the barn raised about three inches when along came a haole. The haole asked, "What are you doing?"

Manuel and Joaquin explained that their mule's ears kept hitting the top of the door, so he wouldn't go in. So they were raising the barn so the mule's ears wouldn't hit the top of the door.

"Well," said the haole, "you're doing it the hard way. It'd be a lot easier if you dug a ditch and then walked the mule into the barn in the ditch." The haole then went on his way.

Manuel turned to Joaquin and said, "What a dummy. Anybody can see that it's the mule's ears too long, not his legs."

"Do you file your fingernails?" Joaquin asked.
"No," said Manuel, "I throw them away."

How did Mary cure her husband of chewing his fingernails?

Had all his teeth pulled.

Freddie Babooze went into Waikiki and sat next to a tourist in a bar. The tourist said, "Let's play a little game. I'll ask you a riddle and if you can answer it, I'll buy you a drink, but if you can't answer it, you buy me a drink." Freddie said that sounded right.

The tourist said, "My parents had one child. It wasn't my brother. It wasn't my sister. Who was it?"

Freddie scratched his head for a minute and said, "I give up. Who was it?"

The tourist said, "It was me!" Freddie said, "I guess the joke is on me," and he paid for a round of drinks.

That night, Freddie was drinking with Manuel in a bar in Kalihi. He told Manuel, "I got a game. If you can answer a question, I'll buy you one drink. No can answer, you buy me one drink. Yah?"

Manuel said okay and Freddie said, "My parents had one child. It wasn't my brother. It wasn't my sister. Who was it?"

Manuel scratched his head and gave up.

Freddie laughed and said, "It was some tourist in Waikiki."

Did you hear about the Portagee who got stranded on an escalator during a power outage?

HOW DO YOU KEEP A PORTAGEE MAN BUSY?

(over)

HOW DO YOU KEEP A PORTAGEE MAN BUSY?

(over)

Little Maria was in school and her teacher asked, "Maria, how do you spell farm?"

Marie wrinkled her brow, thinking. Then after a while, she began to rock back and forth and her lips were moving silently. Finally she cried out, "E-I-E-I-O!"

What does a Portagee say on a postcard?

"Howzit. Having a good time. Where am I?"

Manuel and Joaquin decided to become truck drivers and went to take their driving test. Manuel asked what he would do if he was driving down the Pali Highway and the brakes failed.

He said, "I'd wake my partner up. He's never seen a bad wreck before."

Do you know why the Portagee spent three days in the revolving door?

He couldn't find the doorknob.

The doctor told Manuel that if he wanted to get well he had to do what he said and drink lemon juice after a hot bath. Manuel said he'd try.

A week later Manuel went back to the doctor. The doctor asked, "Did you follow my instructions?"

Manuel said, "I tried, Doc, but I just couldn't do it. By the time I finished drinking the bath, I was too full to drink the lemon juice."

Manuel and his brother walked into a bar in Waikiki and were asked by the bartender, "Do you know what has four arms, four legs, two heads and is really stupid?"

Manuel and his brother shook their heads and said no.

"It's you and your brother," said the bartender.

The brothers decided to pull the joke on someone else, so they went to another bar where they met another two drinkers.

Manuel said, "Do you know what has four arms, four legs, two heads and is really stupid?"

The drinkers shook their heads and said no.

Manuel grinned and said, "Me and my brother."

What do you call a Portagee in a tree?

A branch manager.

"Father," said little Manuel, "I flunked the geography test today because I couldn't remember where the Azores are."

Manuel's father said, "Son, if you're going to succeed in life, you must remember where you put things!"

Freddie Babooze went skydiving with his friend Manuel. Freddie jumped first, counted to ten, pulled the rip cord and his chute opened.

Manuel jumped next, counted to ten, pulled the rip cord and . . . nothing happened. Manuel was falling quickly. He pulled the emergency rip cord. Again nothing happened. Manuel kept dropping and soon he passed his friend Freddie.

Freddie saw his friend go by and began unbuckling his chute. He shouted, "You want to race, do you?"

Do you know the hardest part about being a Portagee in the summer?

Driving around with the windows rolled up so the neighbors think you have air-conditioning.

29

Freddie Babooze and Maria Tunta got married and spent their wedding night at the Royal Hawaiian Hotel. The groom kissed his bride and then rolled over and went to sleep.

"Ey," said the bride, shaking her new husband awake, "this our wedding night. I thought we'd go farther than this."

So Freddie got out of bed, packed, checked out of the hotel, and drove Maria to the Turtle Bay Hilton.

Manuel and Joaquin were talking. Manuel said, "I drove by your house last night and saw you kissing your wife in the window."

Joaquin said, "The joke's on you. I wasn't even home last night."

Two Portagees were drinking in a Waikiki bar and one of them asked, "Do you think Don Ho is his real name?"

The other Portagee thought about the question and sipped his drink, then said, "Do I think whose real name is Don Ho?"

How come Portagees can't make Kool-Aid?

They can't figure out how to get a quart of water into the little envelope.

The bartender asked Manuel what he wanted to drink.
Manuel said, "I think I'll have a 13."
"What's that?" the bartender asked.
"That's a Seagram's 7 and a 7-Up, you dummy."

Manuel and Joaquin went fishing off the Kona coast on the Big Island and caught plenty fish. When it was time to return to shore, Manuel said, "We got to mark this spot so we can fin' 'um next time we go fishing." The spot was marked and they started for the dock.
When they arrived, Manuel asked Joaquin, "You sure you mark the spot?"
Joaquin said, "Yes, I sure!"
Manuel asked, "Okay, Mr. Wise Guy, how you mark the spot?"
Joaquin said, "I put a X on the boat."
Manuel said, "Stupid! What happens if we don't get the same boat next time?"

How do you get a one-armed Portagee out of a coconut tree?

You wave at him.

Why don't stores give their Portagee employees more than half an hour for lunch?

They don't want to have to retrain them.

A policeman stopped Freddie Babooze on Kalanianaole Highway and told him, "You were driving on the wrong side of the road."
Freddie said, "I know that. But the other side was full."

Three Santa Clauses on the roof. Which one is the Portagee?

The one in the bunny suit.

Manuel was visiting his rich friend, who took him on a tour of his mansion. The friend was bragging about his furniture. He said, "That dresser goes all the way back to Louis the Fourteenth."

Manuel said, "Well, I'm in the same boat. If we don't make a payment, our furniture goes back to Sears the fifteenth."

Freddie Babooze was sent into space with a monkey.

On the first day, a red light went on and the monkey took down all the instrument readings.

On the second day, the red light went on again and this time the monkey made all the appropriate calculations.

On the third day, a green light went on.

Freddie snapped to attention and said, "What's that mean?"

"Feed the monkey," said a voice from Earth.

How can you identify the groom at a Portagee wedding?

He's the one in the clean bowling shirt.

After he retired, Freddie Babooze decided to take up a new hobby and raise chickens. He went to a hatchery and bought 200 baby chicks.

The next week he came back and bought 200 more.

After another week, he was back again to buy another 200 chicks.

The hatchery owner asked him why he came in every week.

"Well," said Freddie, "something seems to be wrong. Either I'm planting them too deep, or too close together."

Why don't they have ice cubes in Kakaako?

They lost the recipe.

Did you hear what happened when Manuel's car was stolen?

When the policeman came, Manuel proudly said, "You won't have any trouble catching the thief. I got the license number."

Why did Maria Tunta drive twice through the car wash?

She liked the special effects, but couldn't understand the ending.

Manuel and Mary were expecting their first baby and as the time approached, Mary started worrying about traffic.

"Just our luck," she said, "the baby's coming and it's rush hour."

Manuel patted her hand and said, "Don't worry, we take two cars. That way, one of us is sure to make it."

Did you hear about the Portagee mosquito?

It bit Dolly Parton on the arm.

"Knock, knock."

"Who's there?"

"Portagee burglar."

Joaquin staggered out of a bar in Waikiki. He saw a tall man in a blue uniform with gold braid and said, "Mister, will you call me a taxi?"

The uniformed man said, "I do not work for this hotel. I am an admiral."

Joaquin said, "Well, then call me a boat."

Did you hear about the Portagee who got a pair of cuff links and a short-sleeved shirt for his birthday?

He had his wrists pierced.

How can you tell a Portagee computer operator?

He's the one with all the White Out on the screen.

How do you keep a Portagee busy?

Put him in a round room and tell him there's $100 in the corner.

Manuel ran into another car in traffic, denting the fender slightly. The second driver was angry and he pulled Manuel out of his car and stood him up in the middle of the road and drew a circle around his feet in chalk.

"You stand there, and don't move!" he said. Then the man got a tire iron and went to Manuel's car and smashed the headlights and the windows. Then he put dents on the trunk, the hood, the roof, and the doors. When he finally looked back at Manuel, Manuel was grinning happily.

This angered the man even more and he demanded to know why Manuel was smiling.

Manuel finally stopped grinning and said, "Well, the joke's on you. When you weren't watching, I stepped out of the circle five times."

What's the difference between a rich Portagee and a poor Portagee?

The rich Portagee has two cars jacked up in his front yard.

Manuel and Joaquin were driving out Nimitz Highway to the airport. They saw a sign that said, "Airport Left," so they went home.

Freddie Babooze showed up at work with two bandaged ears.

"What happened?" said Manuel.

"Well," Freddie said, "last night I was ironing my shirt when the phone rang and I picked up the iron by mistake and burned my ear."

"What happened to your other ear?" said Manuel.

"Oh," said Freddie, "I had to call the ambulance."

Did you hear about the Portagee bank--the bank that says, "Huh?"

Did you hear about the Portagee bank--you bring in a toaster and they give you $1,000?

Advertisement from *The Honolulu Advertiser*:
WANTED: Portagees to stand on top of semi-truck to watch for underpasses. Need six per week.

How can you tell there's a Portagee at a cockfight?

He enters a duck.

How can you tell which one at the fight is the Portagee's cousin?

He bets on the duck.

Did you hear about the Portagee who bought a bottle of after-shave lotion and slapped himself to death?

Did you hear about the man who was half Portagee and half Italian?

He made himself an offer he couldn't understand.

What's Portagee car insurance called?

It's called "My Fault."

A haole, a popolo, and a Portagee came to Hawaii looking for jobs. The haole and the popolo got work right away, but weeks went by without the Portagee finding employment. Finally he told his roommates that he had an interview for a TV commercial in the morning. So he set the alarm and went to bed.

In the middle of the night, his roommates smeared black shoe polish over his hands and face and then moved the clock ahead, so that when it went off, the Portagee thought he was late. He leaped out of bed, pulled on his clothes, and rushed to the interview.

The interviewer said he was sorry, but the person had to be white. "But I'm white," the Portagee in black-face said. "My name is Freddie Babooze."

"I'm sorry, Mr. Babooze," the interviewer said, "but the part in the commercial calls for a Caucasian."

"But I'm not black!"

The interviewer said, "You may not think you're black, but have you looked in a mirror lately?"

Freddie went to a mirror nearby and said, "Oh, my goodness . . . they woke the wrong guy!"

Why do the Japanese, the Pakes, and the Portagees all walk with tiny steps?

The Japanese wear tight dresses. The Pakes are tight. And Portagees forget to cut the string holding the slippers together.

Manuel, Joaquin and Freddie had locked themselves out of their car. Manuel suggested working a
coat hanger inside the window to lift the button up.
Joaquin said that would take too long. He suggested
getting a crowbar to force the door open. Freddie said,
"I don't care what you do, but you better hurry up,
because it's starting to rain and the top is down."

Manuel asked his friend to stand in front of his car
and tell him if his directional blinker lights were
working.
Joaquin said, "Yes . . . no . . . yes . . . no . . . yes . . .
no . . . yes . . . no . . . ."

Freddie Babooze was hired to paint the center
stripe down the middle of Farrington Highway. The
first day he completed three miles, the second day two,
and the third day only one.
His boss made an inspection and called him over.
He said, "Hey, Freddie, how come the first day you
paint three miles, the second day you paint two, and
the third day you only paint one? You lazy, or what!"
Freddie shrugged and said, "I just kept getting
farther and farther away from the can of paint."

Did you hear about the Portagee who wouldn't go out with his wife because he heard she was married?

When the U.S. Surgeon General came out with a report that said cigarette smoking caused cancer in mice, the Portagees put their cigarettes high up on a shelf, where the mice couldn't get them.

Did you hear about the Portagee who willed his body to science?

Science is contesting the will.

What do you call someone who tells the punchline first and then the joke?

A Portagee comedian.

DA BLALLAH
& DA TIDAH

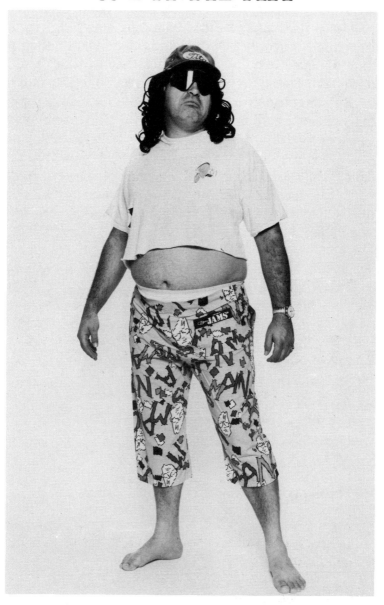

Da Blallah

Back in the late fifties there was a young local boy who emerged from the slums of Honolulu to become a rock and roll star. His first language was pidgin and he wrote his deeply personal and meaningful music in that dialect. In spite of the fact that no one could understand what he was saying, he had one smash hit.

But tragedy struck one day while he was driving his Volkswagen bug down Makapuu side on his way to a concert down Waimanalo Beach Park. His car flew over the cliff, got caught in one Japanese ulua fisherman's sugi line and sank to the bottom. He died.

But he left us with one island rock and roll classic that will live forever. His name: Itchy Valenz. The hit: "Da Blallah."

I'm a bla bla bla bla blallah
I'm a bla bla bla bla blallah
No boddah me
I stay Halekauwila
I work body and fendah
Stay live my car
My honey's place
My muddah's house
I stay eat Tasty Broilah
You no go mess with my sistah
I slap your head
I broke your nose
I bust your face
Blallah, Blallah
Blallah, Blallah
Blallah, Blallah

I'm a bla bla bla bla blallah
I'm a bla bla bla bla blallah
No boddah me
I make da kine big body
I like listen da radjo
Make any kine
Make any kine
Make any kine

There may be some of you unfamiliar with this local dialect. So, in fairness to you and to this sensitive song about the life of a local boy, we have translated it for you.

I'm a bla bla bla bla blallah
    (I am a large local fellow)
I'm a bla bla bla bla blallah
    (I am a large local fellow)
No boddah me
    (But it is of no consequence)
I stay Halekauwila
    (I frequent Honolulu's industrial district)
I work body and fendah
    (I am an automotive design specialist)
Stay live my car
My honey's place
My muddah's house
    (I have various places of residence)
I stay eat Tasty Broilah
    (Among my interests is gourmet dining)
You no go mess with my sistah
    (Please don't compromise my female siblings)
I slap your head
    (It does not sit well with me)
I broke your nose
    (And I can be very convincing)

I bust your face
   (Would you still like your ears in their present
   position?)

I'm a bla bla bla bla blallah
   (I'm a rather tall part-Polynesian male)
I'm a bla bla bla bla blallah
   (I'm a rather tall part-Polynesian male)
No boddah me
   (But it is of no consequence)
I like make da kine big body
   (I take self-improvement courses)
I like listen da radjo
   (I admire Beethoven and other classical
   composers)
Make any kine
   (I have a wide variety of interests)
Make any kine
   (I engage in a great range of activities)
Make any kine
   (I have a wide variety of interests and engage in
   a great range of activities)

Blallah, Blallah
Blallah, Blallah
Blallah, Blallah

Luceel

In one bar in Kalihi
I saw this wahine
She sat down and hemo'd her ring
I was all smelly
But still was niele
So I asked her, "Hey, chick, what's your thing?"
She was all bust up
Cause she started to cuss up
She said, "I'm fed up to here
My old man is lazy
He's stupid, he's crazy
And I think I'm going have one more beer"

I then spocked his shadow
Was more big den one cattle
I checked to see where he was at
He moved towards the lady
Who was right next to me
He seemed da kine nervous, like dat
He had more muscles showin'
Than twenty Samoans
For a second I thought I was dead
But he started shaking
Cause his heart was stay breaking
He turned to the Tidah and said,
"WHAT! LUCEEL! YOU GOING LEAVE ME
NOW?
"THE KIDS NEVER EAT YET! MANGO SEASON
NOT PAU!
"I KNOW MY CAR SMOKIN'! AND DA STEREO
STAY BROKEN!
"BUT, WOW! LAU LAU!

47

"WHAT! LUCEEL! YOU GOING LEAVE ME NOW!"

> After he split us
> I order two Millers
> I thought how she made him make A
> We then left da bar
> And got into my car
> I still nevah know what for say
> She tried for make scandal
> But I couldn't handle
> She must have thought I was da kine
> She said, "Brah, you're handsome"
> But I never like chance um
> Cause da words was still fresh on my mind
> "WHAT! LUCEEL! YOU GOING LEAVE ME NOW?
> "THE KIDS NEVAH EAT YET! MANGO SEASON NOT PAU!
> "I KNOW MY CAR SMOKIN'! AND DA STEREO STAY BROKEN!
> "BUT, WOW! LAU LAU!
> "WHAT! LUCEEL! YOU GOING LEAVE ME NOW!"

NOTE: The word Blallah comes from the word Bruddah, pidgin English for Brother. When a boy goes through puberty, he gets a disease called "Blallah-itis," which is a growing pains disease. If he doesn't grow out of this bully-ish, arrogant WOT-WOT! attitude as an adult, he becomes a Blallah--no respect for others and others' property, and no respect for himself. Same thing for Tidah. Tidah comes from Tita, which is pidgin English for Sister, or Sistah. Without proper supervision and love, these unfortunate people become Blallahs and Tidahs.

What are the three most difficult school years for a Blallah?

Second grade.

What do you call a 22-year-old Tidah in the fourth grade?

Gifted.

This big Blallah walked into a bar in Kalihi with a pit bull on a leash and said, "Do you serve Miller draft?"

The bartender eyed the pit bull nervously and said, "Yes, we do."

The Blallah then asked, "Do you serve Portagees?"

The bartender said, "Yes, we do."

"Good," said the Blallah. "I'll have a draft and a Portagee for my dog."

Why do Blallahs have small steering wheels on their cars?

So they can drive with handcuffs on.

Why do you have to put a fence around a field when playing a Blallah team?

So the Tidah cheerleaders won't graze.

What do you call one Tidah and six pit bulls?

A fair fight.

What do you call a Blallah hitchhiker?

Stranded.

Why does Hawaii have Blallahs and Tidahs and California have earthquakes?

California got first choice.

When a Tidah marries a Blallah, how can you tell them apart?

If one of them has a mustache, that's the Tidah. But usually you can't tell them apart. They both have big arms, mustaches, and cracked heels.

Definition of a Blallah car pool: Six Blallahs carrying a pickup truck to work.

A Tidah walked into a Waikiki bar carrying a duck under her arm.

"Hey," said the bartender, "you can't bring a pig into this place."

"This no pig," said the Tidah, "this a duck."

The bartender said, "I was talking to the duck."

PERSONAL AD: "Blallah farmer, 40, desires meaningful relationship with woman 30-35 who owns tractor. Send picture of tractor."

Describe a Blallah marriage proposal.

"You're going to have a WHAT?"

A Blallah, a Filipino, and a haole were arguing at the beach park about who had the smartest and strongest dog. They decided to meet again the next day with their dogs to see which one could perform the most impressive stunt.

Next day, the haole showed up with a German shepherd, the Filipino with a Doberman, and the Blallah with a pit bull.

"My dog's name is Duke," said the haole. "You see that canoe over there and that small island in the ocean? Duke will paddle the canoe around the island and back again." The haole said, "Go, Duke!" and the dog launched the canoe and paddled it around the island. As a reward, the haole gave the dog a bone.

"That's nothing," said the Filipino. "My dog's smarter and stronger than that. You see my pickup over there? Samson will turn it into a mini-truck for cruising." The Filipino signaled his dog and Samson installed hydraulic cylinders that caused the truck bed to rise and fall, tinted the windows, installed a boom box, and painted the vehicle lavender. As a reward, the Filipino gave the dog a bone.

"So you think your dogs are so smart!" said the Blallah. "Watch what my dog does." So saying, the Blallah turned to his pit bull and said, "Go for it!" The pit bull went over to the other two dogs, killed them and ate them, then took the two bones and left for lunch.

What do you get when you cross a Tidah with a Pake?

Ug Lee.

What do you get when you cross a Blallah with a Tidah?

Injured.

What do you get when you cross a Tidah with a Korean?

A hostess with the mostes'--and nobody refuses to buy her a drink.

What do you get when you cross two Blallahs?

Injured.

What do you get when you cross a pit bull with a poodle?

Not a very good watchdog, but a really vicious gossip.

How can you tell a Tidah?

You can't. Best to keep your mouth shut altogether.

What's the difference between an elephant and a Tidah?

Twenty pounds and a muumuu.

What's the difference between a Tidah and a pit bull?

Lipstick.

What do you get when you cross a Tidah with a pit bull?

A dog with two attitudes.

What do you say to a Blallah businessman?

Nothing. There aren't any.

Did you hear about the Tidah who was a light eater?

She started eating as soon as it got light.

What's a Blallah's seven-course dinner?

A six-pack and poke.

What do Blallahs do on their day off?

Same old t'ing.

A Blallah named Henry saw a long procession moving down the street toward the cemetery. The parade consisted entirely of men and was led by another Blallah leading a pit bull on a leash. Henry went up to the Blallah and said, "Forgive me, brah, but this one strange funeral. Would you mind, who's it for?"

The Blallah with the pit bull said, "It's for my mother-in-law." He looked at his dog and said, "My pit killed her."

"Oh, that's terrible," said Henry. "But . . . uh, could you lend me your dog for a day or two?"

The Blallah nodded and pointed his thumb over his shoulder and said, "Get in line."

DA BUDDHA HEAD

Slant Eyes

Although I'm proud I'm a Japanee
Sometimes it's very hard to see
My eyes are always at a squint
It's just like reading tiny print
That's Japanese optometry

CHORUS:
Oh, slant eyes!
It is not accidental
Slant eyes
It's just that we are Oriental
Slant eyes.

It's just like looking through a slit
Our contact lenses cannot fit
They either think we are sleeping
Or that we are peeping
We cannot make our eyelids split

We can look right through venetian blinds
We like to stare at power lines
It's easy to look under beds
To look at trees we turn our heads

If you Asian, that's the way it goes
Your eyes are open when they're closed
It's hard, but then again
You could be an Arabian
With open eyes and slanted nose

NOTE: Japanese were first called Buddha Heads back in plantation days. It was a friendly term, used by friends. Today it is a pidgin English word and some Japanese take offense.

One fellow said to another, "I heard the Arabs are going to buy up all of the property in Hawaii.

The other said, "Don't worry, the Japanese will never sell it."

Four men were in a life raft. One was Russian, another was Cuban, the third was Hawaiian, and the fourth was Japanese.

The Russian took a swallow from a full bottle of vodka and threw the rest overboard.

The Hawaiian said, "Ey! You waste a lot of vodka that way."

The Russian said, "Where I come from, we have lots of vodka."

Next, the Cuban took a puff from a huge cigar and then threw the cigar into the water.

Again the Hawaiian cried out. "Ey! Give me the cigar next time."

The Cuban said, "Where I come from, we have lots of cigars."

So the Hawaiian picked up the Japanese and threw him overboard."

Did you hear, the Japanese have their own version of "The Mickey Mouse Club"?

The way the song goes now, it's spelled, "M-I-C-K-E-Y G-U-C-C-I."

Did you hear? They've renamed Kahala.

Now it's called Kahara.

How does a Japanese tourist spell relief?

R-O-L-E-X.

Did you know that 85% of all Japanese men have Cataracts?

The rest drive Rincolns.

What's a Japanese tourist look like?

A cross between Louis Vuitton and Mickey Mouse.

DA SOLE

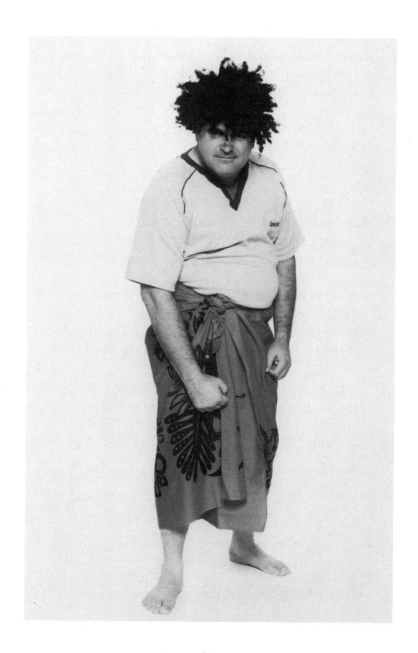

Abdullah Fataai

I'm nine feet tall and six feet wide
I got a neck made of elephant hide
I scrape da haoles off the soles of my feet
I drive my Volkswagen from the back seat

CHORUS:
Abdullah, Abdullah Fataai
Abdullah, Abdullah Fataai

I eat green bananas, tree and all
My favorite game is tackle football
I wear a skirt, but you better not laugh
Cause it won't be funny when I break you in half

I'm as gentle and sweet as a grizzly bear
Only difference is he got more hair
I have the largest muscles on all of Oahu
Next to King Kong, King Kong look mahu

I got the nicest smile in all the Pacific
I got an island home that's super terrific
But I don't like fight and you don't like die
So when I say, "Talofa!" you better say, "Hi!"

NOTE: *Samoans call each other "Sole." Period.*

There are no Samoan jokes.

When you're telling jokes, you have to be careful who you're telling them to. You can't joke about a haole's religion---haoles are very sensitive about their religion. A Hawaiian, you can't joke about the land, the 'aina. The Hawaiians are very sensitive about the land.

Now, Samoans, you can't joke about anything. No sense of humor dem.

The coach wasn't happy with his team. The football season was half over and they had a 0-6 record. He wondered if the plays were too complicated and decided to make them very simple. So before going into the seventh game, he gave them only four calls: SRR, SRL, SPDS, and HBK.

"Wha's that mean?" one of the Samoan players asked.

The coach explained, "SRR stands for Samoan Run Right. SRL means Samoan Run Left. SPDS means Same Play, Different Samoan. And HBK means Haole Boy Kick."

What do you call a haole surrounded by three Samoans?

Doomed.

What do you call a haole surrounded by five Samoans?

Coach.

What do you call a haole surrounded by ten Samoans?

Quarterback.

What do you say to a Samoan in a business suit?

"Will the defendant please rise?"

Why has there never been a report of a shark attacking a Samoan?

Fear.

How can you tell a Samoan cigarette girl in a night club?

She's the one carrying the cigarette machine under one arm.

What do you get when you cross a Samoan with a haole?

Nothing. There are some things even a Samoan won't do.

DA BUK BUK

The Purple Danube

What's purple and brown, buk-buk, buk-buk
What squats on the ground, buk-buk, buk-buk
Holds knife to your throat, buk-buk, buk-buk
And eats billy goat, buk-buk, buk-buk
Who dance with two poles, buk-buk, buk-buk
Has hairs on his moles, buk-buk, buk-buk
Who eats bagoong, all day long
You are right, it's me the manong

Who drives Cadillac
Light show on the back
Who wears silver pants
Goes out disco dance
Who works on Lanai
Who's wife is hapai
Who mixes opai with fish eye
You are right, it's the P.I.

Who owns fighting cock
Who wears orange socks
Who owns barber shops
Who cannot grow chops
Who greases his hair
Who perfumes the air
Who has funny lips, no more hips
You are right, it is the Flips.

NOTE: Filipinos in the plantation days in Hawaii had a joke they used when someone had a cavity, a round hole in the front teeth. The Filipino would tease that person by pointing to that hole and yelling out, "Buk-buk, buk-buk!" "Buk-buk" means "termite" and the joke means the termite ate a hole in the teeth. Why do we include "Buk-buk" in pidgin English? Because others from other ethnic groups saw the early Filipinos pointing at each other and calling "Buk-buk!" and thought that was what they called each other. It developed in the plantation days, when pidgin English was developing.

If a Filipino is a Buk Buk, what do you call Filipino children?

Buklets.

If a Filipino is a Buk Buk, what do you call Waipahu?

A library.

What do you get when you cross a Filipino with a Czechoslovakian?

A Czech Buk.

What do you get when you cross a Filipino with a Portagee?

A blank buk.

What do you call a banquet table of Filipinos?

An encyclopedia.

Did you hear about the new Filipino cookbook?

101 Ways to Wok Your Dog.

What do Filipinos call a dogcatcher's truck?

Meals on Wheels.

What's a Filipino's favorite meal?

Mutt loaf.

There were two Filipinos appearing on "That's Incredible." One had car insurance. The other was an only child.

What do you call a Filipino failure?

A flip flop.

Do you know why Filipinos are so short?

So they don't have to bend over when they make the beds.

Why are there no Filipino doctors?

Because you can't write prescriptions with spray paint.

What is the most difficult decision a Filipino has to make before going to a formal party?

Whether to wear his red socks or his green socks.

What's red, green, blue, yellow, purple, and orange?

A Filipino businessman.

What's red, green, blue, yellow, purple, and orange and dances?

A Filipino pickup truck.

What do you call a Filipino family without a dog?

Vegetarians.

What do you call a Filipino family with one dog?

A family that doesn't know where its next meal is coming from.

What do you call a Filipino family with five dogs?

Ranchers.

Official Filipino bird: Fighting chicken.

Why aren't there any Filipino astronauts?

Because they'd want to paint the capsule green, honk the horn, squeal the tires, and play the radio too loud all the way to the moon.

Did you hear about the Filipino bride who wore something old, something new, something borrowed, something blue, something orange, something green, something lilac, something chartreuse, something red, something . . . ?

How can you identify the bride at a Filipino wedding?

She's the one with bicycle reflectors all over the bodice of her dress.

Eduardo went to UH to learn English. First, he learned vocabulary. The teacher said, "Please use 'tenacious' in a sentence."

Eduardo thought for a minute, scratched his head. Then he said, "Ebery morning, before I go to school, I bend down and tie my ten-ay-shoos."

The teacher next asked Eduardo to use the word "window" in a sentence.

Eduardo got that one right away and said, "Win do we eat?"

Finally the teacher said, Please use the following four words in a sentence: 'deduct . . . defense . . . defeat . . . and detail.'"

Eduardo was quiet for a long time and finally he said, "De duck jumped ober de fence, de feet before de tail."

What's the one thing you can count on in Waipahu?

Your fingers.

DA PAKE

Bruce Spring Roll

Born down in a Chinatown
First buck I made was selling char siu bao
My father was a gambler, always out of luck
My mother was a waitress at the Golden Duck

CHORUS:
I was born . . . a tight Pake
Born . . . a tight Pake
I was born . . . a tight Pake
I was born . . . a tight Pake
I was born . . . a tight Pake

Now at the Golden Duck they call me the boss
I fire my own mother just to keep down the cost
I yell at my employees and I never say t'anks
And I keep all my money in the Liberty Bank

I was born . . . a tight Pake

I was born . . . a tight Pake

I was born . . . a tight Pake

I was born . . . a tight Pake

Did you hear about the new brand of tires, Pakestone?

They not only stop on a dime, they pick it up.

What's the difference between a Pake and a canoe?

Canoes occasionally tip.

Why did the Pake cross the road?

To open another store.

A group of Pake businessmen decided to start Pake Airlines. After talking it over, they offered three classes of travel.

In First Class, they show a movie and serve steak and lobster.

In Coach Class, they show slides and give you a chicken dinner.

In the "No Frills" section, they pass around a picture of a peanut butter sandwich.

How do Pake mothers name their babies?

They throw some silverware down the stairs and name them after the noise it makes.

What do Pakes do on their day off?

Inventory.

How do you get ten Pakes into a Volkswagen?

Throw in a dime.

What's a matched set of Pake luggage?

Two shopping bags from Foodland.

How is Christmas celebrated in a Pake home?

They put parking meters on the roof.

How do you blindfold a Pake?

Dental floss.

Wong was a notorious tightwad, and to make himself feel better, every day on the way to his office he gave a quarter to the poor woman who sold manapua on the street corner. He never took a manapua, but always dropped a coin in her hand, feeling himself a virtuous man.

This continued for about six months when the woman called after Wong as he left. "Mister . . . mister . . . I got to tell you something."

Wong stopped and said, "I bet you want to know why I always give you a quarter, but never take a manapua, don't you?"

"No," the woman said. "That's your business. It's my business to tell you that the price went up to thirty-five cents."

Did you hear about the Pake marine?

Gung Ho.

Did you hear about the sick Pake?

Heave Ho.

What do you get when you cross an Italian with a Pake?

Don Ho.

What's the Pake key to success?

The one that fits the Mercedes.

DA YOBO

Korea

Korea, I just met a girl from Korea,
Her hand upon my knee, her breath smells like kim
chee, to me.

Korea, I just met a girl from Korea,
She picked up all my coin, her hand upon my groin, oh
gee!

Korea, with my money wrapped 'round my finger,
Keeps her hand there and just lets it linger.
Korea, Korea, Korea, Korea.

Korea, I'm stuck with this girl from Korea,
She says her name is Kim, I pray she's not a him, a he.

Korea, she no wear a brassieah.
She works at Misty II, does what the bar girls do, to
me!

Korea, she don't talk much but calls me honey.
She won't stop 'til she's got all my money.
Korea, Korea, Korea, Korea.

She's a countrified girl who comes from Seoul.
Korea!

NOTE: *Koreans are sometimes called Yobo. This comes
from the Korean greeting, "Yobo seyo." Today, some people
think the word has a negative meaning, yet in Korea, "yobo"
means sweetheart.*

How many Korean barmaids does it take to open a bottle of champagne?

None. Their Japanese and haole customers open it for them.

What are the four things you are most likely to find in a "Korean" bar?

Hawaiian pupus, American booze, a Japanese karaoke room, and Vietnamese hostesses.

What do you get when you cross a Korean bar girl with an elephant?

A two-ton pickup.

What do you get when you cross a Korean bar girl with a pit bull?

A waitress with an offer you can't refuse.

What is the favorite choice of birth control for Korean bar maids?

Two jars of kim chee before bed.

What do you get when you cross a Yobo with a Pake?

A shopper who always gets a bargain by asking the shopkeeper, "Hoooooowwwww much did you say that was?"

What do you get when you cross a Korean bar maid with a pit bull?

Answer #1: A better-looking waitress.

Answer #2: A friendlier waitress.

What do you get when a Yobo marries a Japanee?

Four angry parents.

THE HAOLE

Haoles Anonymous

I'd like to talk to you seriously now, if I may. There is a social problem in Hawaii that is prevalent, but which few are willing to talk about. It's a condition that some of us have that's easy to recognize but extremely difficult to cure. There are symptoms and I am about to tell you a few of them. Listen carefully. I may be talking about you.

Do you use Number 57 sunscreen? Do you order mashed potatoes with your teri beef plate? Do you think the Brothers Cazimero are a pair of Hispanic trapeze artists?

If you've answered yes to any one of these questions, then you must face the sobering truth: you are . . . HAOLE!

Do not be frightened. Do not be scared. This condition--also known as the Caucasian Complex or the Honky Syndrome--has been successfully treated. With the help of "Haoles Anonymous," Caucasians have learned to live healthy, productive local lives. There are hundreds of recovered haoles walking the streets of Hawaii today thanks to this special support group. Let me introduce you to one right now.

ANNOUNCER: Before Haoles Anonymous . . .

"Hello. My name is Brad. Haoleness ran in my family. My mother was a haole, my father also. I live in the Waialae-Kahala district of Honolulu. I voted for Fred Hemmings in the last election . . ."

ANNOUNCER: After Haoles Anonymous . . .

(Forced pidgin) "How is zit, brah. My name Brad. I eat loco moco for breakfast. I engage in conversation with . . ."

ANNOUCER (whisper): Talk story . . .

"I talk story with mokes and . . ."

ANNOUNCER: Titas . . .

"Titas."

See, within a few sessions, even hardcore haoles can learn to function in local society.

Caucasians Are Strange People

CHORUS:
Caucasians are strange people
Caucasians are strange, strange people
Caucasians are not like you and me

It's like they come from another planet
Their skin gets red when they try to tan it
They wear plaid socks, plaid shirts, plaid pants
They call their uncles "unks" and their aunties "aunts"
They talk too fast and they laugh too loud
They embarrass you when you're in a crowd
They got lots of friends and lots of money
They think Andy Bumatai is funny

Don't want no Caucasians, don't want no Caucasians, don't want no Caucasians around here.

If you are at a party and everybody is hanging out, drinking beer and grinding aku poke, and you jump up and say, "Anybody want to play charades?" you are . . . HAOLE!

If your toes overlap from being in shoes too long, you are . . . HAOLE!

If you like pasta salad, but not macaroni salad, you are . . . HAOLE!

CHORUS:
Caucasians are strange people
Caucasians are strange, strange people
Caucasians are not like you and me

They're smarter than you and smarter than me
But they can't tell sushi from sashimi
Their men wear a size 14 shoe
They don't put tomato sauce in their stew
They'll eat kalua pig, but they won't touch poi
They always talk about life in Illinois

Don't want no Caucasians, don't want no
    Caucasians, don't want no Caucasians around
    here.

If your name is Bruce, or Rick, or Betsy, or Laura,
you are . . . HAOLE!
    If you look older than you really are, you are . . .
HAOLE!
    If old Japanese men hate your guts, you are . . .
HAOLE!

CHORUS:
Caucasians are strange people
Caucasians are strange, strange people
Caucasians are not like you and me

They buy aloha pants for their aloha shirt
They eat a Japanese dinner and they want dessert
They'll spend two weekends in Lahaina
And then call themselves a kamaaina
Their face, arms, legs, nose are all too long
They think "Tiny Bubbles" is a Hawaiian song
They put two pads of butter on their two scoops
    rice

They eat snow cones, but not shave ice
Don't want no Caucasians, don't want no
    Caucasians, don't want no Caucasians around
    here.

NOTE: Haole is a Hawaiian word. It means "foreigner," especially a white person. Captain Cook was the first white person to come to Hawaii. The Hawaiians had never seen white people before, so they thought he was a god. In the Hawaiian language, "ha" means "to breathe" and "ole" means "not" or "without." So "haole" means "without breath."

What do you call a haole in Waianae?

A fool.

What do you call a haole on his second visit to Waianae?

A slow learner.

Did you hear that the alligators in Florida wear little haoles on their T-shirts?

What do haoles call perfect sex?

Simultaneous headaches.

Why did God invent golf?

So haoles could dress up like Filipinos.

How many haoles does it take to change a light bulb?

Six. One to call the electrician, and five to write the environmental impact report.

Why did God invent haoles?

Somebody has to buy retail.

What's a haole's idea of open-mindedness?

Dating a Canadian.

How can you tell when it's a haole wedding reception?

The Pake caterer at the end of the line is handing out one finger sandwich and one glass of champagne per person.

Why did the haole cross the road?

To get to the middle.

How can you tell the haoles in a Pake restaurant?

They're the ones not sharing the food.

Two haoles were drinking at the Waialae Country Club. One turned to the other and said, "You know, you're my best friend and you never ask me how I'm doing, how things are going, how's business?"
"Okay," said the friend, "how's business?"
"Fine."

DA MIXED PLATE

I'm Local

I'm local: L-O-C-A-L!
As brown as one dollar-size opihi shell
I'm as local as the ume in your musubi
As one spaghetti plate lunch with side order kim
    chee

I'm as local as the gravy on the three scoop rice
As all the rainbow colors on da kine shave ice
I'm as local as one B-1 cockaroach
Flying for your face in one ewa approach

As local as one five-foot south shore swell
As the tree at the Halekulani Hotel
As the hotel room with the kamaaina price
As Auntie Alexine when she make nice nice

CHORUS:
I'm the life of the land
I'm the son of the sea
I'm the child of the rock
Rockchild

I'm as local as a '69 Volkswagen bug
With the black tinted glass and the remnant rug
I'm as local as the noodles in your saimin soup
As one 200-pounder in a hula hoop

I'm as local as the mustache on Waihee's face
As one Hawaiian-style band with one electric bass
I'm as local as one Tidah with homemade tattoos
As one first-class, A-1, high-grade babooze

I'm as local as the Maunakea Street lei stand
With the haku, money, Lifesaver lei--three strand
As one Kamehameha grad with one haole face
As one second-grader who forgot his race

CHORUS:
I'm the life of the land
I'm the son of the sea
I'm the child of the rock
Rockchild

I'm as local as the swap meet down at Kam Drive-
    In
As the huli huli chicken papaya skin
I'm as local as one passion-orange Popsicle
As the tilapia in the pool at the capitol

I'm as local as the bubbles inside Primo beer
As local as the Heftel campaign smear
I'm as local as the droppings from one Molokai
    mule
As da kine pidgin English in the public school

I'm as local as the fat in Auntie Vern's lau lau
As the bricks in the church called Kawaiahao
I'm as local as the splinters in one split chopstick
As one Japanese surfer with one haole chick

CHORUS:
I'm the life of the land
I'm the son of the sea
I'm the child of the rock
Rockchild

I'm as local as the campers down Kahana Bay
As the mayor when he says, "Eh, make my day!"
I'm as local as the mango that stay out of reach
As all the naked babies down Waimanalo Beach

I'm as local as one certified shaka sign
As one brand new Cane Haul Road design
I'm as local as one hotel union strike
As one Sacred Falls three-mile hike

I'm as local as the guy is down in O-triple-C
As one Chinee, Filipino, haole, Portagee
I'm as local as one moke down Nanakuli side
I'm as local as one lying tourist guide

CHORUS:
I'm the life of the land
I'm the son of the sea
I'm the child of the rock
Rockchild

What do you get when you cross a Blallah with a Pake?

A car thief who can't drive.

What's the Vietnamese national anthem?

"Shrimp Boats Are A-Coming."

What do you get when you cross a Portagee with a Filipino?

A teenager who spray-paints graffiti on a chain link fence.

What do you get when you cross a Portagee with a Pake?

Someone who saves all his money, but can't remember why.

Three men died in an airplane crash--a haole, a Pake, and a Blallah--and all three went to Hell. The Devil was in a good mood and he told them that for $20 each, they could return to life. The haole paid his $20 and suddenly he was back on Earth, where his wife threw her arms around him and thanked God. Then she asked him, "Where are the other two?"

The haole said, "I don't know. When I left, the Pake had the Devil down to $15 and the Blallah said he was waiting for his welfare check."

The World's Shortest Books

Portagee Wit and Wisdom

Japanese Manners

Blallah Millionaires

Low-Cal Plate Lunch Recipes

Famous Pake Philanthropists

Famous Blallah Pacifists

Tidah Hair Styles

Big Hawaiian Landowners

Characters Left Out of
James Michener's Novel About Hawaii

Kimo Therapy

Saimin Legree

Terry Yaqui

Pua Ting

Lei Down

Masa Kerr

Lynn Ching

Kim Chee

Mo Chee

To a haole, XXX means a dirty movie.

To a banker, it's three Blallahs co-signing a note.

To a Tidah it's a tee-shirt size.

The son of a Pake and a Blallah approached his parents with a problem: was he more Pake than Blallah, or more Blallah than Pake?

His parents asked him why he wanted to know. He said there was a kid in the neighborhood who had a bicycle he wanted, and he wanted to know if he should try to bargain him down on the price, or steal it.

A Portagee, a Filipino, and a haole jump off the roof of a hotel in Waikiki. Who lands first?

Answer #1: The haole, because the Filipino stopped to spray-paint graffiti on the walls, and the Portagee stopped to ask directions.

Answer #2: Who cares?

In what neighborhood on Oahu are three languages spoken fluently at different times of the day or year?

Kahala, where English is spoken at night, Tagalog during the day when the residents leave for work and are replaced by Filipino gardeners and maids, and Japanese during Golden Week.

What's Haunani-Kay Trask's dream?

A million kamaaina haoles swimming back to California with a tourist under each arm.

ORDER BLANK

Please send me _____ copies of
Frank DeLima's Joke Book
@ $9.95 each*.

I am enclosing my check or money
order for $ _____ ,
payable to **BESS PRESS**.

_____
Name (Please print)

_____
Address

_____
City   State   Zip

*Price includes tax and handling charge. Allow
3-4 weeks for delivery. Price subject to change.

BESS PRESS
P.O. BOX 22388
HONOLULU, HI 96823